DIY Science Experiments for Kids

DIY Science Experements for kids

© All rights reserved. No part of this book may be reproduced or used in any manner without the prior written permission of the copyright owner, except for the use of brief quotations in a book review.

Lesson #1:
DIY Volcano

Materials:
- Baking soda
- Vinegar
- A small plastic bottle
- Modeling clay
- Red food coloring

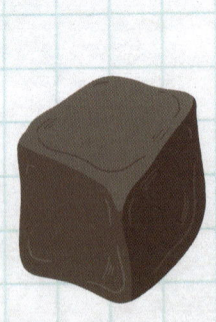

Create a volcano shape around the bottle using modeling clay.

Add a few drops of red food coloring and a tablespoon of baking soda inside the bottle

Pour vinegar into the bottle, and watch the volcano "erupt" with bubbles.

How did the experiment go?

Expectations:

_____
_____

_____
_____

Observations:

_____
_____

_____
_____

Lesson #2:
Homemade Slime

Materials:
- Mixing Bowl

- White PVA glue

- Starch

- Food coloring (optional)

Mix equal parts glue and starch in a bowl.

Add a few drops of food coloring for colorful slime

Stir until it forms a gooey consistency.

How did the experiment go?

Expectations:

_____

_____

_____

_____

Observations:

_____

_____

_____

_____

Lesson #3:
Static Electricity Butterfly

Materials:
- A piece of paper

- A plastic comb

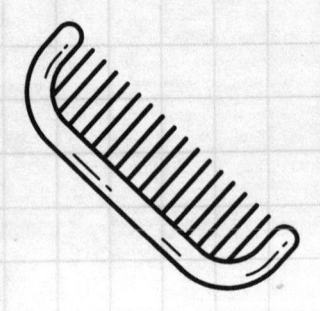

- Small pieces of tissue paper

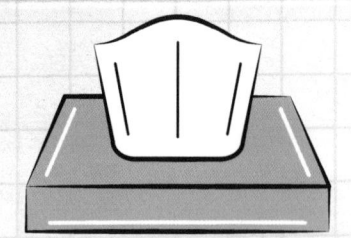

Rub the comb against your hair to create static electricity.

Hold the comb near the tissue paper pieces
Now watch them "magically" stick to the comb, resembling butterflies.

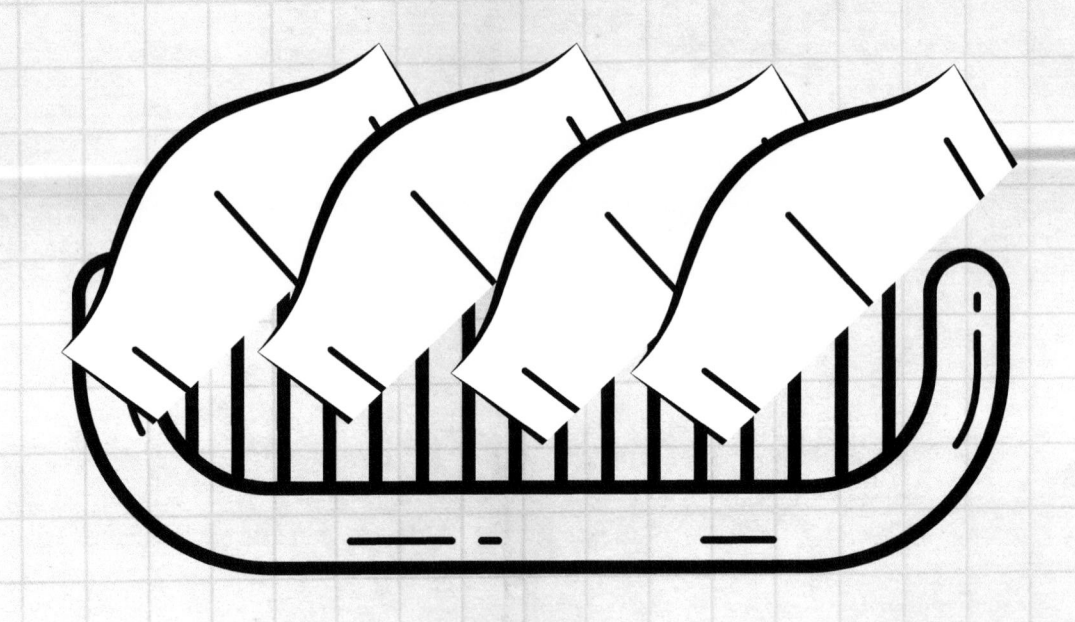

How did the experiment go?

Expectations:

_____
_____
_____

Observations:

_____
_____
_____

Lesson #4:
Rainbow Milk Experiment

Materials:
- A plate
- Whole milk
- Dish soap
- Food coloring (optional)

Pour a thin layer of milk onto a plate.

Add drops of different food coloring colors.

Then, add a drop of dish soap to the center of the milk and watch as the colors swirl and mix, creating a rainbow effect.

How did the experiment go?

Expectations:

_____

_____

_____

Observations:

_____

_____

_____

Lesson #5:
Balloon-Powered Car

Materials:
- A small toy car with wheels
- A balloon
- A straw
- Tape

Tape a balloon to the back of the car, with the open end facing the back

Insert a straw onto the balloon's nozzle

Blow up the balloon, then pinch the end of the straw shut

Place the car on a smooth surface and release the straw to propel the car forward

How did the experiment go?

Expectations:

_____

_____

_____

_____

Observations:

_____

_____

_____

_____

Lesson #6:
Homemade Lava Lamp

Materials:
- A clear plastic bottle
- Water
- Vegetable oil
- Food coloring
- Bubble tablets (Carbonation Tablets)

Fill the bottle two-thirds with vegetable oil and one-third with water.

Add a few drops of food coloring

Drop in a broken Bubble tablet, and watch colorful bubbles rise and fall, creating a lava lamp effect.

How did the experiment go?

Expectations:

_____
_____
_____
_____

Observations:

_____
_____
_____
_____

Lesson #7:
Glow-in-the-Dark Jars

Materials:
- A clear jar
- Glow-in-the-dark paint
- A paintbrush

Paint the inside of the jar with glow-in-the-dark paint.

Charge it by placing it in sunlight or under a lamp,

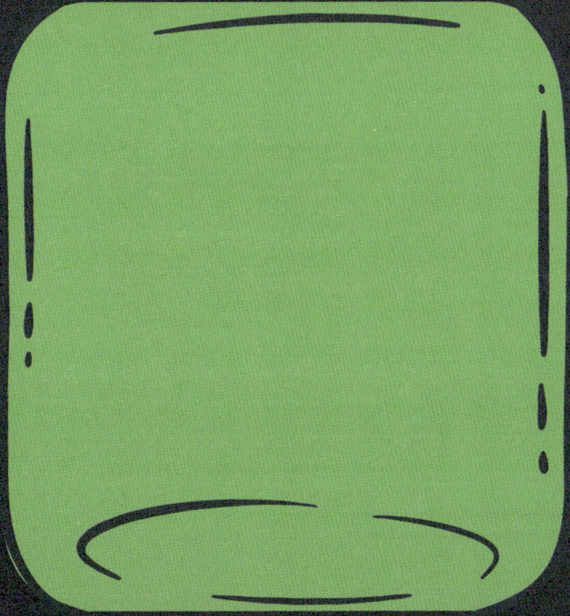

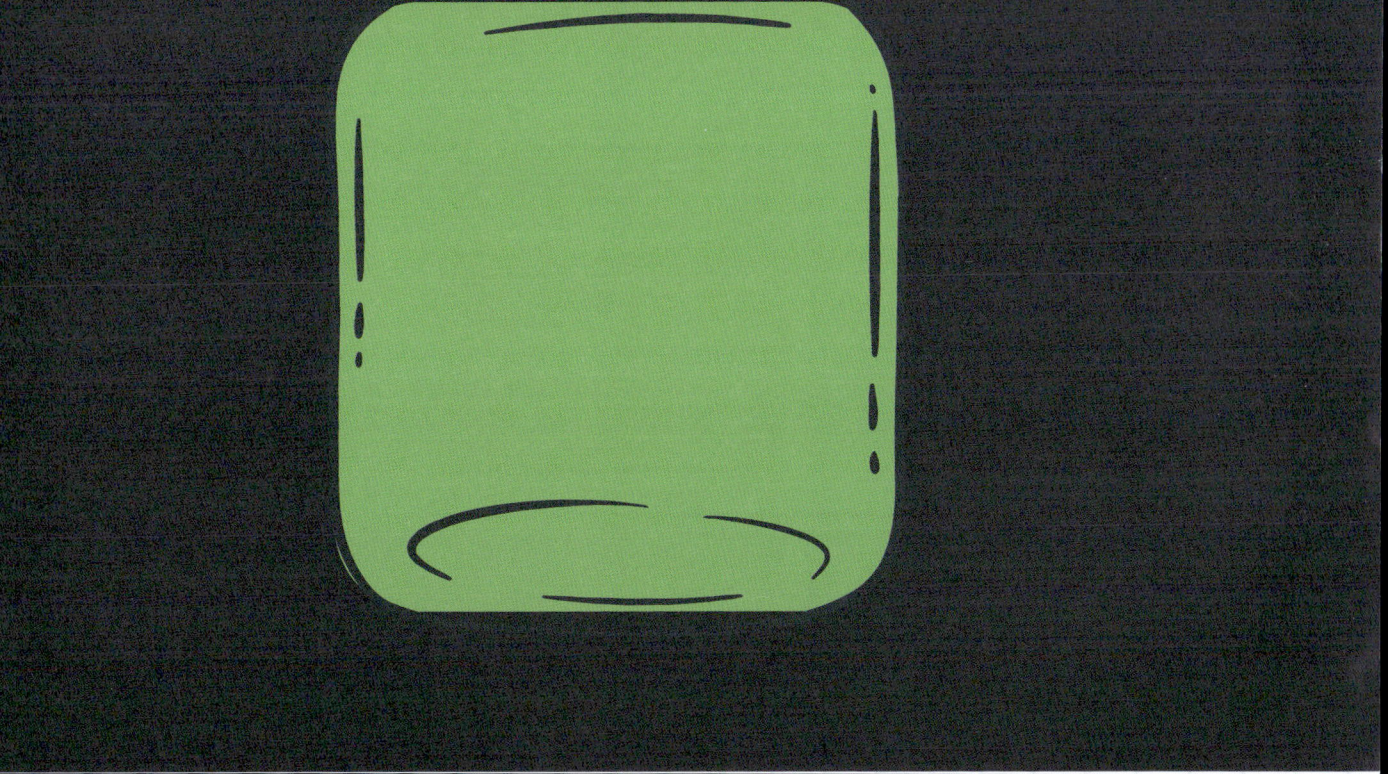

How did the experiment go?

Expectations:

_____
_____
_____
_____

Observations:

_____
_____
_____
_____

Lesson #8:
Potato Battery

Materials:
- A potato 
- Copper (pennies) 
- Zinc nails (paperclips) 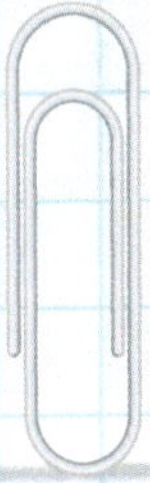
- Wires with alligator clips
- An LED light

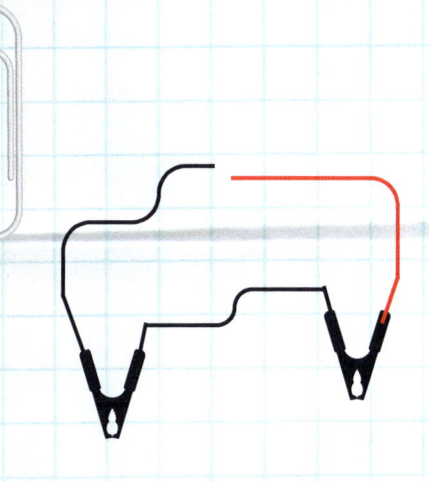

Insert a penny and a paperclip into the potato

Attach wires with alligator clips to each nail and connect them to an LED

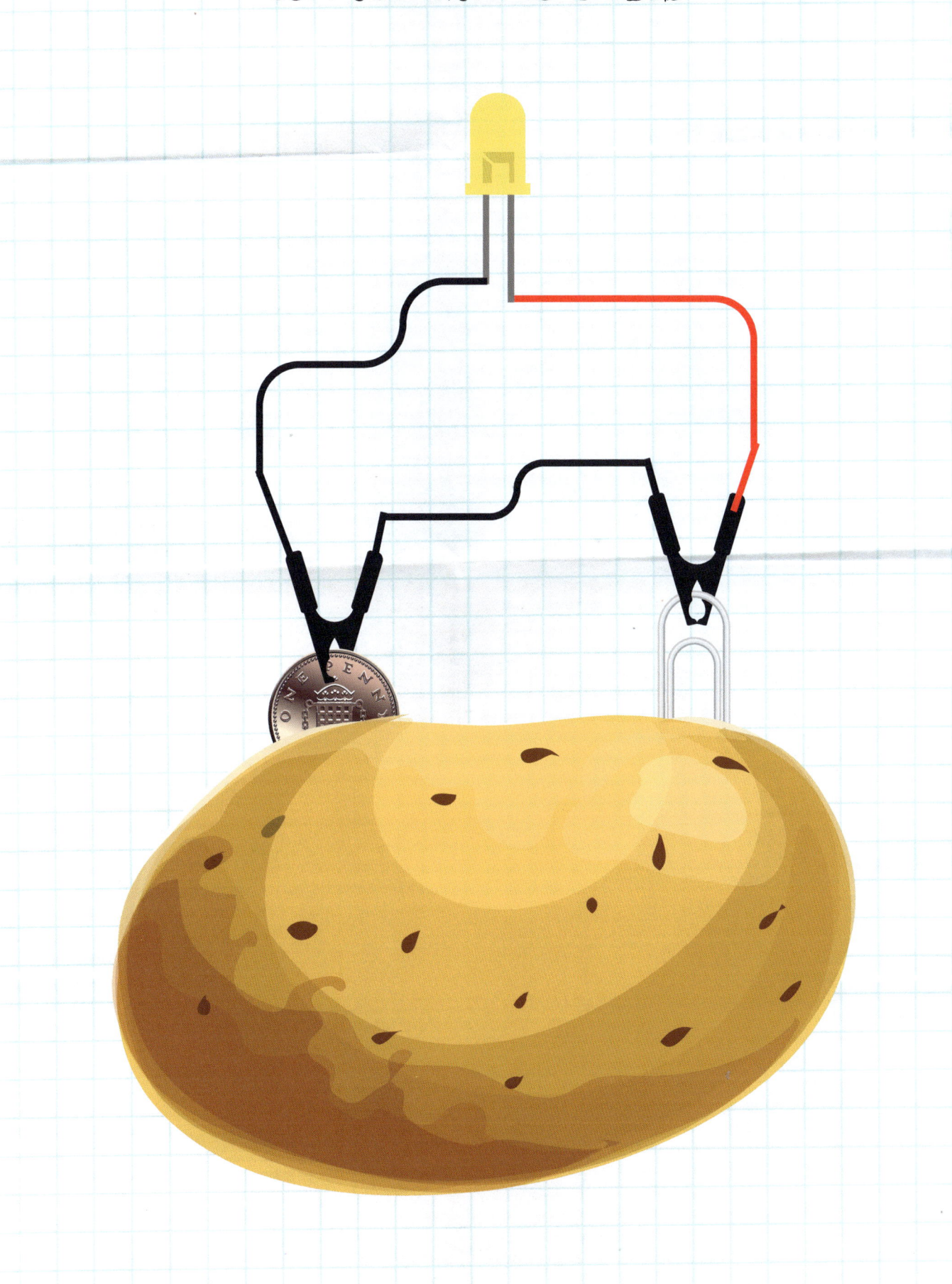

The potato battery will make the LED light up.

How did the experiment go?

Expectations:

_____

_____

_____

Observations:

_____

_____

_____

Lesson #9:
Invisible Ink

Materials:
- Lemon
- White paper
- A cotton swab
- A heat source (e.g. a light bulb or an iron)

Use a cotton swab to write a message or draw a picture on the white paper using lemon juice

\+

Let it dry completely.

To reveal the hidden message, carefully heat the paper (with adult supervision) using a light bulb or an iron set to a low temperature.

I like science!

How did the experiment go?

Expectations:

_____

_____

_____

_____

Observations:

_____

_____

_____

_____

Lesson #10:
Egg in a Bottle

Materials:
- A hard-boiled egg
- A glass bottle with a narrow neck
- A piece of burning paper or a match.

Light a small piece of paper or a match (adult supervison) and drop it into the bottle.

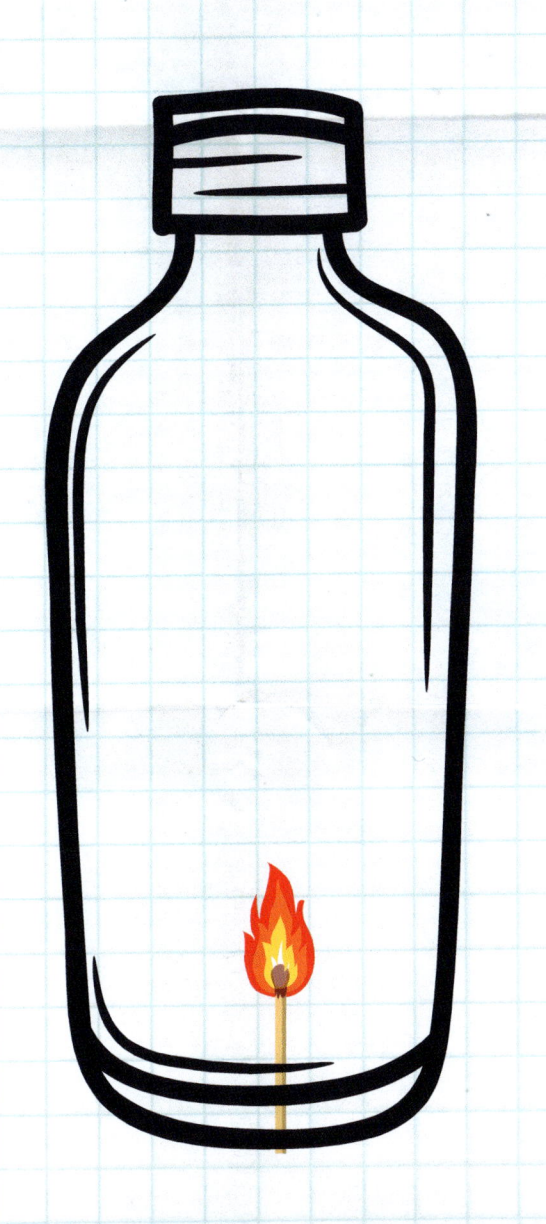

Quickly put the egg on the mouth of the bottle, and watch as the egg gets sucked into the bottle due to changes in air pressure.

How did the experiment go?

Expectations:

_____

_____

_____

Observations:

_____

_____

_____

Lesson #11:
Baking Soda and Vinegar Balloon Blow-Up

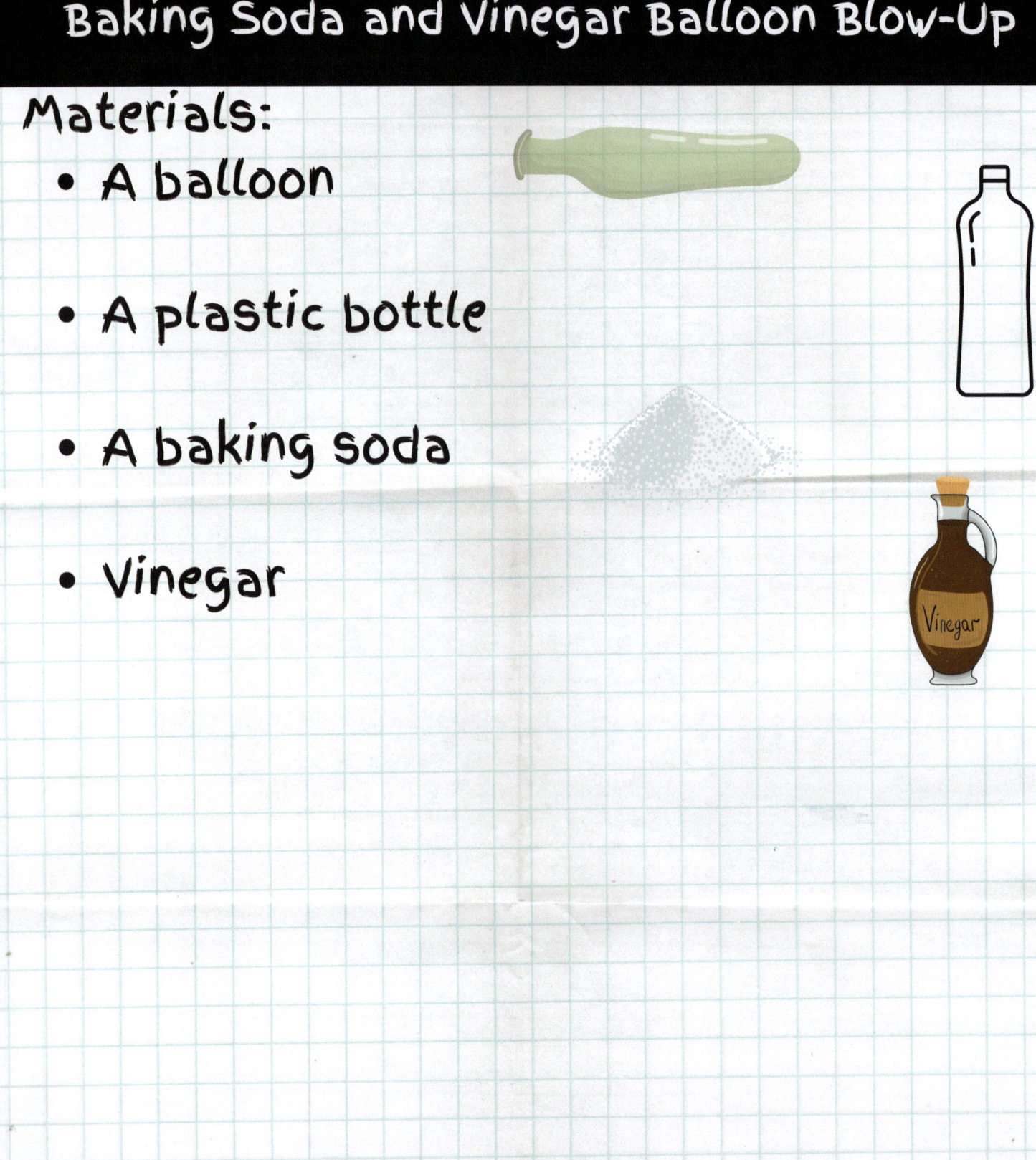

Materials:
- A balloon
- A plastic bottle
- A baking soda
- Vinegar

Put a few tablespoons of baking soda into the deflated balloon.

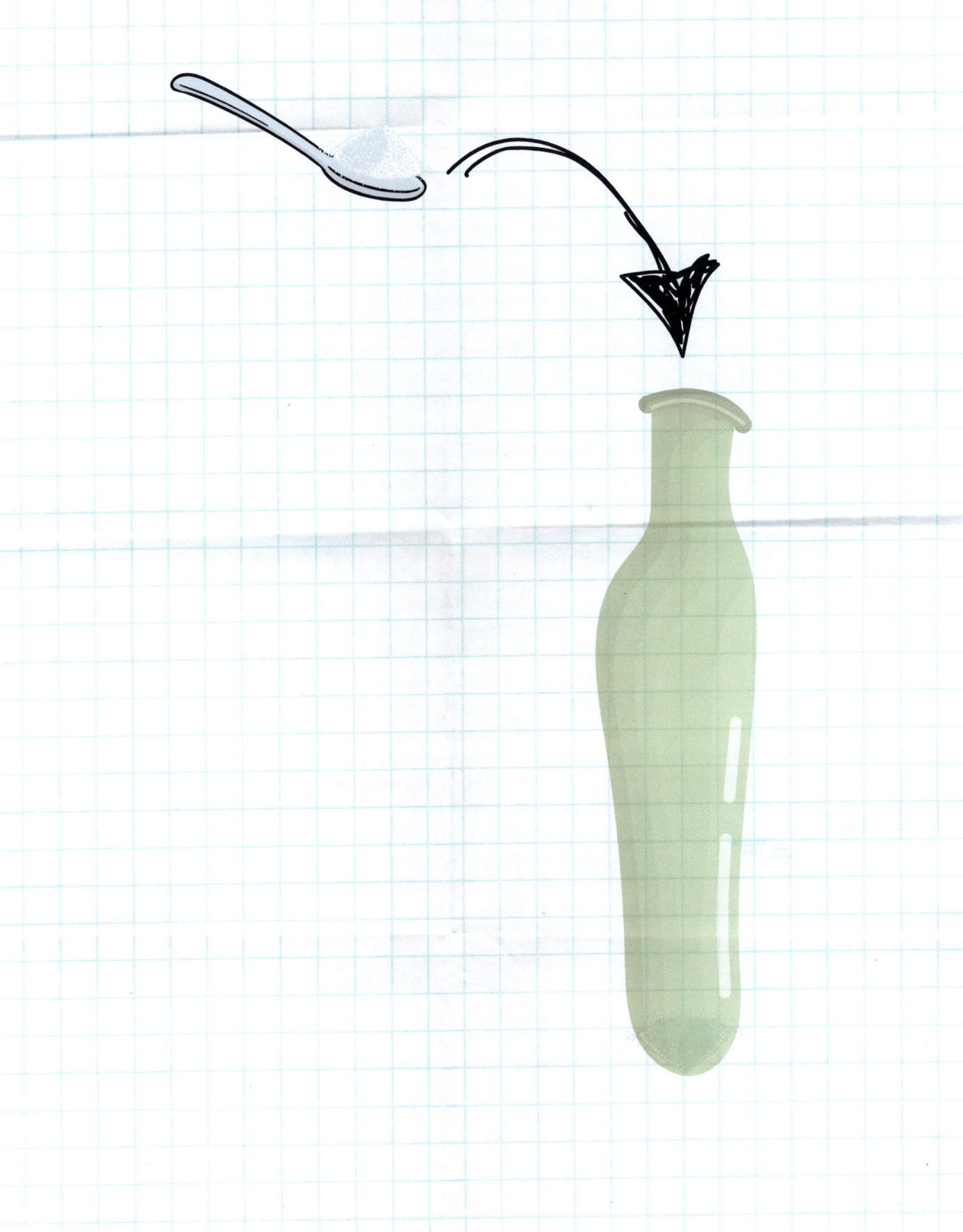

Pour vinegar into the bottle, attach the balloon to the neck of the plastic bottle without letting any baking soda fall inside the bottle.

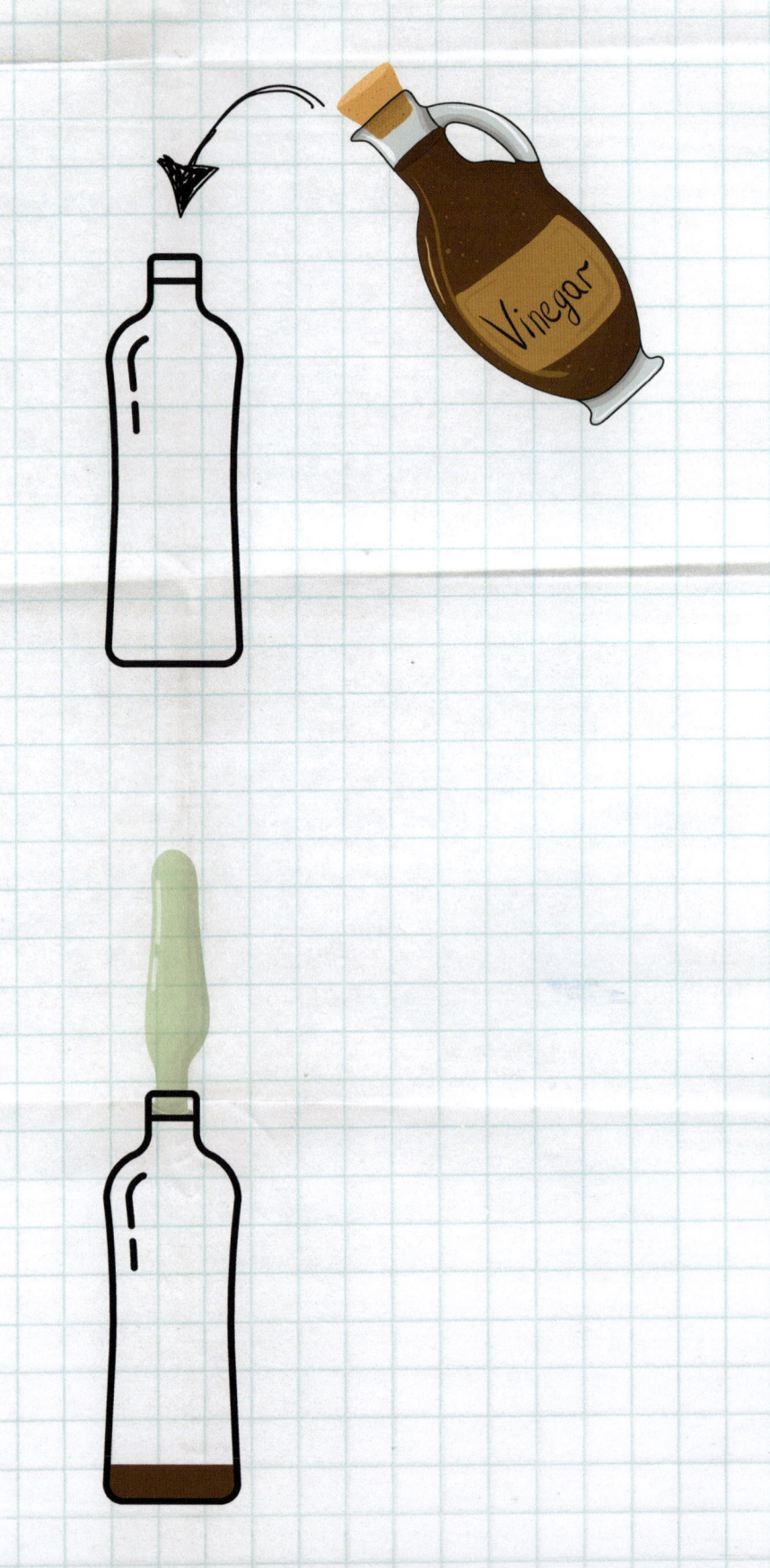

Tilt the ballon so the bakign soda falls into the bottle. Watch as the balloon inflates as the vinegar reacts with the baking soda.

How did the experiment go?

Expectations:

_____

_____

_____

Observations:

_____

_____

_____

Printed in Great Britain
by Amazon